Living Green

Walking, Biking, and Riding the Bus

By Meg Gaertner

level 2 little blue readers

www.littlebluehousebooks.com

Little Blue House is distributed by North Star Editions:
sales@northstareditions.com | 888-417-0195

Produced for Little Blue House by Red Line Editorial.

Photographs ©: Shutterstock Images, cover, 4 (top), 4 (bottom), 7, 8–9, 10–11, 12 (top), 15, 17, 18, 20–21, 22–23, 24 (top right), 24 (bottom left), 24 (bottom right); iStockphoto, 12 (bottom), 24 (top left)

Library of Congress Control Number: 2022901879

ISBN
978-1-64619-602-9 (hardcover)
978-1-64619-629-6 (paperback)
978-1-64619-680-7 (ebook pdf)
978-1-64619-656-2 (hosted ebook)

Printed in the United States of America
Mankato, MN
082022

About the Author

Meg Gaertner enjoys reading, writing, dancing, and being outside. She lives in Minnesota.

Table of Contents

train
car

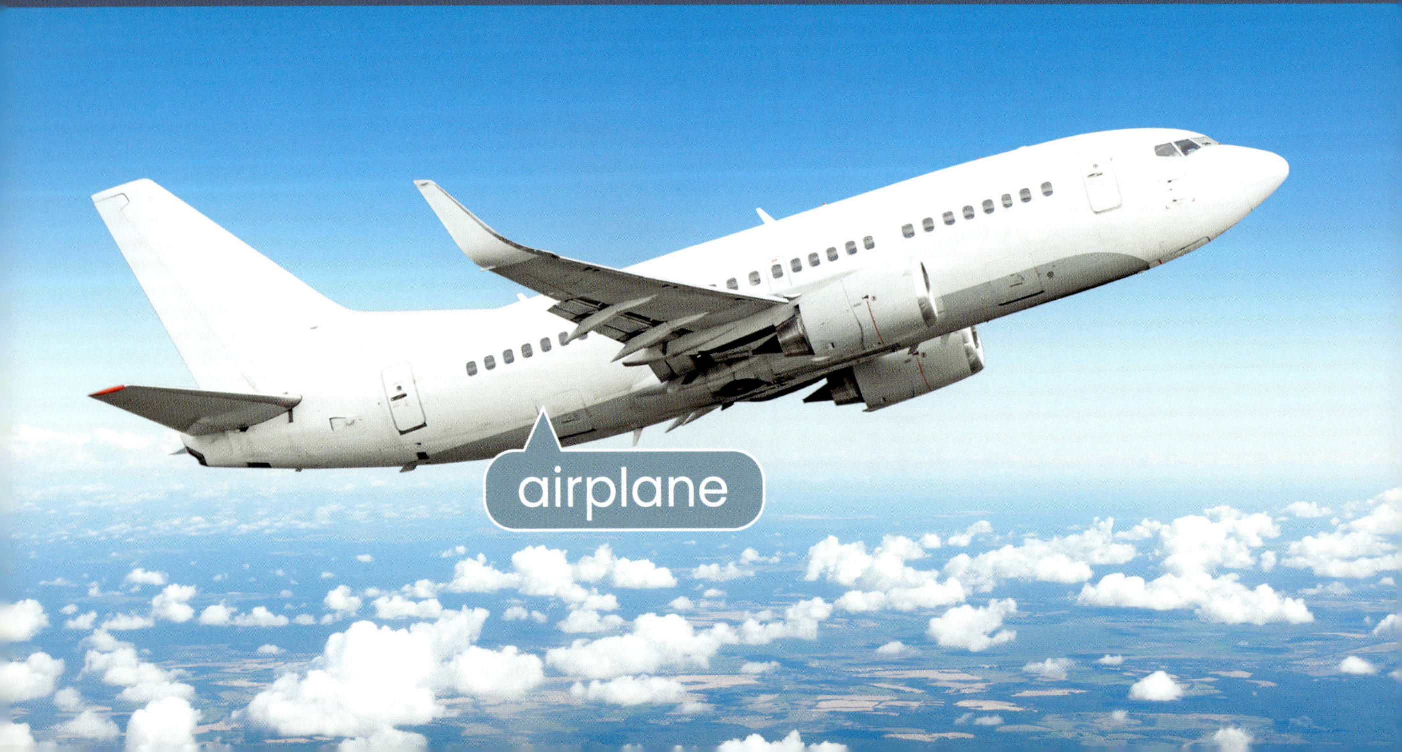
airplane

Moving Around

People move from one place to another in many ways. They can drive cars, take trains, or fly in airplanes. These ways require energy.

For example, most cars and airplanes use fuel. Burning fuel makes energy for movement.

Making and burning fuel puts harmful gases into the air.

These gases make the air dirty, and they are unhealthy to breathe.

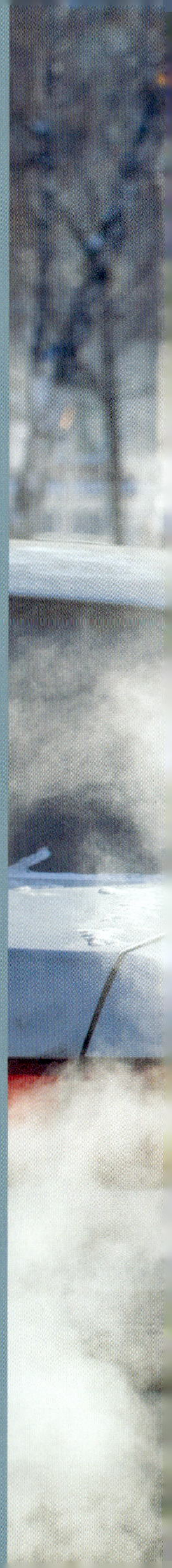

gases

But people do not always need cars or airplanes. Other ways of traveling are cleaner for Earth. They are also better for people's health.

walking

biking

Walking or Biking

Sometimes people walk or bike to school or work. Both are good exercise, too. They also do not harm Earth.

Some places have a walking school bus. A group of children walk together to school. An adult walks with them to keep them safe.

walking school bus

Do you live close to your school? Ask an adult if you can start a walking school bus in your neighborhood.

bus
В 437 ТУ 02 RUS

Riding the Bus

People can also ride the bus
to get around.
Buses drive the same roads
every day.

Buses burn fuel but carry more people than cars. So, buses use less energy for each person. Buses are better for Earth than cars.

With an adult's help, learn about the buses in your neighborhood. Can you use a bus to get to school?

SCHOOL BUS

Glossary

biking

walking

gases

walking school bus

Index